Living the Amish Way

Seven Essential Amish Values to Enrich Your Life

Ramsey Coutta

ISBN 9781798469491

Table of Contents

Foreword

There is something about the way of life and character of the Amish that draws us to them. Since the first immigrants set foot on the shores of the future United States of America, society has been constantly changing. At one point in our history Amish society and general American society were virtually indistinguishable. However, as time passed American society transformed in unimaginable ways, much of it based on tremendous industrial and electronic progress. While America changed, the Amish observed these changes and even participated in some of them. Eventually though, the Amish came to recognize that to change with modern American society meant to sacrifice and lose most of their cherished Christian beliefs, values, and practices. In response, the Amish began saying no to many of the changes they were witnessing. As a result, much of Amish culture remained the same while American society took on a whole new look and feel. The cultural divide between Amish and general American society became wider and wider and continues to grow even today. Many Americans now look upon the Amish with bemused curiosity unable to understand why the Amish are the way they are.

While most Americans would not be unwilling to give up their modern conveniences, the Amish have said no to most. The reasons are primarily spiritual in nature and revolve around maintaining a close knit community. As a result, the Amish live in a manner that is more akin to turn of the 18th century America rather than the 21st century. Americans who observe such a way of life in comparison to their own find it quaint and amusing. But when they find out more about who the Amish are and what they believe they also begin to feel as if something significant and important is missing from their own life. What this is is not easy to put a finger on but concepts such as community, simplicity, family, purpose, joy and love often come to mind. The

Amish have not only managed to hang on to a way of life that is simple and uncomplicated, but they have also managed to hold on to those values and relationships that many moderns find missing from their life and long for.

Whereas once the Amish were reviled for their way of life, now they are applauded by many. However, the Amish are not perfect and they know it. Every culture has its own set of positives and negatives and those who are part of the culture often know these best. The Amish recognize many of their own deficiencies, but when they look at the alternative of giving into living like modern Americans most choose to stay Amish. They choose to remain faithful to those core values that have served them so well for so long.

This book is about seven of those Amish core values that help to make them who they are. Of course the Amish have more core values than seven, but these are the ones I have determined after my research are particularly meaningful and vital to the Amish way of life. The structure of this book it to look at each value in three parts. The first third of each chapter seeks to describe and explain the value as understood and practiced by the Amish. The second third of each chapter examines the biblical basis for the core value, and the final part of each chapter offers suggestion of how you can live more like the Amish way without necessarily becoming Amish yourself. I hope that after reading *Living the Amish Way* you will in some small way become a better person for it. I know in my study of the Amish I have.

Separation

The Amish place great emphasis on being separate and different from the world around them. The reason comes from both scripture and community experience. Biblical verses such as, *"Wherefore come out from among them, and be ye separate, saith the Lord"* (2 Corinthians 6:17) and *"Be ye not conformed to this world, but be ye transformed by the renewing of your mind"* (Romans 12:2) are but two among many in the bible that direct Christians to be separate and different from unbelievers. The Amish don't take such verses as mere suggestions but as admonitions to be faithfully followed.

The Amish experience life in this world as a spiritual struggle[1] and seek to separate themselves and otherwise be different from those aspects of the world that threaten their faith. The "world" to the Amish, primarily refers to the society in which they exist and which they struggle against.[2] A person who is not Amish or of an Amish sect or

Mennonite is considered by the Amish to be worldly.[3] While the Amish recognize that they have to live "in" the world, they try not to live how the world lives and seek to separate and differentiate themselves from it according to scriptural guidance. To the Amish, this struggle is a struggle for the very purity of the church. Their fear is that once the church becomes impure by the influence of the world then it will have lost its willingness and ability to faithfully serve the Lord. They are mindful of the scriptural warning in Luke 14:34-35, *"Salt is good; but if the salt has lost its flavor, how shall it be seasoned? It is neither fit for the land nor for the dunghill, but men throw it out."*

The Amish recognize that being separate and different does not come without community and personal sacrifice. This sacrifice can range from the mildest form of personal inconvenience, due to the lack of modern technology, to wholesale community persecution by a society that is unwilling to tolerate their beliefs and practices. In fact, before the Amish came to America, they experienced years of cruel persecution, torture, imprisonment, and death in Europe in the 16th and 17th centuries as part of the generally despised Anabaptist movement.

In their personal experience the Amish have observed the erosive effects of modern society on their way of life. As a result they seek to have as little to do with it as they can. From sons and daughters who have succumbed to the enticements of the world and left the community to whole families of Amish who have splintered off and become "English" like in their ways of living and worship, the Amish accept they are in a spiritual struggle for the hearts and minds of their own. The worldly system that promotes individualism, relativism, and fragmentation is a serious threat to their values of conformity, Scriptural authority, and community integration.

In the mind and practice of the Amish, "worldly" is a label they use that evolves over time and applies to changes, products, practices, and beliefs that threaten the welfare of their community.[4] As a result, anything that comes to be labeled worldly by the Amish community is held at arm's length. Of course, there are various Amish communities in numerous locations so what is worldly in one group may not necessarily be so with another.

While avoiding certain practices and products of modern society, the Amish also separate themselves in other distinctive and readily observable ways. Some of these involve their language, dress, and mode of transportation. The Amish speak English and a German dialect known as Pennsylvania German or Pennsylvanian Dutch. They primarily use the German dialect for family, friendship, play, worship, and intimacy.[5] They use English in communicating with the non-Amish world around them. They also dress very plainly in muted colors and clothing that covers nearly all of the body for the sake of modesty. Their dress is highly uniform in relation to others in the Amish community. They also travel in the distinctive horse and buggy except for limited times when they may hire more modern transportation. All of these and more serve to effectively separate the Amish from the broader modern society around them.

The practices of separation and differentiation have served the Amish well over the years. As society has transformed dramatically over the past couple of centuries, primarily due to changes in technology, many distinctive groups and sects have lost their distinctiveness and become indistinguishable from the society around them. The Amish recognized early on the danger of these changes to their community and way of life and have steadfastly resisted in a decidedly non-confrontational way. As a result, they have maintained their distinctive customs and practices, but more importantly their spiritual convictions that underlie these.

Be Ye Separate

The non-Amish Christian believer can spiritually benefit from a deeper understanding of the scriptural injunction to be separate and different from the world. The word "separate," in the sense emphasized by the Amish, means to set apart. The Amish seek to set themselves apart from the world in order to avoid being set apart from God. They are mindful of the words of warning Christ spoke to John in Revelation 3:15-16, *"I know not your works, that you are neither cold not hot. I could wish you were cold or hot. So then, because you are lukewarm, and neither cold nor hot, I will vomit you out of my mouth."* An unwillingness as a believer to set yourself apart from the world followed by serving God will eventually lead to a separation of you from Him.

From the very beginning of time, God by His works has proclaimed the good of separation in certain instances. By this I mean He has purposefully separated His Creation according to its distinctive form and function. For example, in Genesis God separated the light from the darkness, the heavens from the earth, the various types of plants and animals from one another, as well as woman from man. It is clear that God's intention is that there be a separation based on differences between some things and others. One possible reason is that His creation functions better this way and more effectively fulfills His will.

While God initiated separation based on physical function at the beginning of time, most other references to separation in the bible are for spiritual reasons. In Leviticus 20:26 God says to the people of Israel, "*And you shall be holy to me, for I the Lord am holy, and have separated you from the peoples that you should be Mine.*" God felt it essential that His people be separate from those peoples they came in contact with in order to maintain their distinctiveness and purity. Apparently, He knew that in order for them to be and remain holy He needed to set them apart from the other peoples, otherwise they would be subject to corruption.

Another example is the command to separate the clean from the unclean people in Leviticus 15:31, "*Thus you shall separate the children of Israel from their uncleanness, lest they die in their uncleanness when they defile My tabernacle that is among them.*" According to scripture, there is a consequence for remaining un-separated from uncleanness, which is embraced by the world. That consequence is our spiritual death. However, God does not want our spiritual death and desires that we follow His command to separate ourselves from all that is unclean.

Nehemiah 13:3 is an excellent example of what the Christian believer's response is to be to God's command to separate from the world: "*So it was when they had heard the law, that they separated the unmixed multitude from Israel.*" Previously, God told the children of Israel that they were not to mix with the Ammonites and Moabites since these groups had earlier resisted the Israelite's march into Canaan and the Moabites had hired Balaam to curse Israel. In response to hearing the law anew, the Israelites removed the Ammonites and Moabites from among them. It's reasonable to believe that if they did not have the power to do this they would have removed themselves instead.

While it's important for the Amish to be separate from the world it is equally, if not more important, for them to become and remain *united* with God. This is a lifelong process that begins in early childhood as they are taught the precepts of the bible. The culmination of this training is when young Amish men and women choose to be baptized and join the church. They are then united with God, the

Amish church, and the Amish community. Life after that is a process of seeking to remain close to God and raising their own family to love God as they were taught.

Paul writes of being united with God in Romans 6:4-5, *"Therefore we were buried with him through baptism into death, that just as Christ was raised from the dead by the glory of the Father, even so we should walk in the newness of life. For if we have been united together in the likeness of His death certainly we also shall be in the likeness of his resurrection..."* As mentioned, baptism is the crowning moment in the earthly life of the Amish believer. Baptism symbolizes dying to sin or being separated from it. One cannot be united with Christ without first being separated from sin.

Jesus also mentioned several times being united with Him. He phrased it as abiding or remaining "in me." For example, in John 15:4 he says, *"Abide in me, and I in you. As the branch cannot bear fruit of itself, unless it abides in the vine neither can you, unless you abide in me."* Here Jesus is emphasizing the importance of permanence and steadfastness in His relationship with the believer and they with Him. A branch can only bear fruit as long as the nutrients from the tree continue to flow to it. The Amish, with their largely agrarian lifestyle, understand the importance of crops continuing to receive the nutrients they need. They recognize that like their crops they too need to continue to receive the spiritual nutrition that only Christ can provide. In order to receive this they have to abide in Him.

Separate Living

Living separately from society in order to remain true to the Christian life that you desire is challenging to your human nature, but after the initial changes you will find it gets easier as you go. Here are several suggestions that should help you to achieve this.

- *First, and perhaps most importantly, know what you want "separation from the world" to look like to you.* It's hard to get somewhere if you don't know where you're going. The Amish know what kind of people they want to be. I won't take the time to list all the details here, but in a nutshell they want to be a people that place God first above all other things and they want to be true to God's commands. So they are willing to rid themselves of anything that threatens to supplant God in their lives or cause them to be disobedient to Him. In the same way, you need to have a clear vision of what being "separate" from the world would look like for you. Make this your guiding vision and begin working toward it. Spend time refining your vision of how you want your life to be "separate" until you clearly know what it is.

- *Identify and begin making specific changes to separate from the world in ways that are spiritually beneficial.* Now the real work begins. Once you know what type of Christian life separate from the world you desire, you must ask yourself what specific changes are needed. Then you must implement these. Perhaps one of these changes is a less intrusive media influence into your home. This might involve getting rid of the TV or perhaps blocking from your television those channels that are the most egregious. It could involve canceling your current cable or satellite provider and subscribing to a Christian provider. Maybe it might mean designating several nights a week media free nights with no TV, radio, or internet and using this time as family time. Identifying and following through with implementation can be challenging, especially if you have to convince others in the home of the importance of making these changes.

- *Set barriers to going back.* Making a change to be more separate from the world will always involve the temptation to fall back into the old ways of doing things. You will find it easier to avoid falling back if you set barriers that make it more difficult to do this. Completely getting rid of something that led you into worldly activities is much more effective than keeping it around the house or apartment and continually being tempted. Completely breaking off ties to a group with sinful and worldly inclinations is much more effective than periodically hanging out with them. A person clinging to a lone rock in a raging sea has to completely let go of it when a life saving rope is thrown by a passing ship or else perish.

- *Get comfortable with the state of being different and making a sacrifice.* Once you begin to making changes to separate from the world your actions are going to start to draw attention. Those closest to you are going to notice the changes first. Depending on how they are affected by these changes, they may react in not so positive ways. This may prove to be difficult for you as you sense them thinking differently of you, but if you are convinced of the rightness of your actions then stay the course. Eventually, you will adjust to the change in perceptions by others. Your changes will also likely cause you and your family to experience a sense of sacrifice over those things you no longer do or participate in. Sacrifice is not easy, but by definition it is not meant to be. However, it will allow you and your loved ones to grow spiritually and you will adjust to the sacrifice to the point that it no longer

feels that way to you.

Simpleness

The Amish are known as a people who live simple and plain lives. This means they choose to do without modern conveniences designed to make life easier or provide entertainment value. If they do happen to have a modern convenience it's not run off the electrical grid but is gas or generator powered. The Amish have observed the impact of modern conveniences on American society and have made determinations whether such conveniences would be harmful to the values they seek to live by.[6] Those modern appliances and conveniences that have the potential to contribute to the breakdown of family and community are simply rejected.

The case of the home freezer illustrates how the Amish have responded to a modern appliance that offers both benefits and drawbacks. Freezers for home use were introduced in the 1950s. These freezers required electricity, which the Amish had previously banned in the

1920s. The Amish who adopted the freezer for personal use powered it from on-site generators. In 1966 the freezer was banned from home use by the Amish because leaders feared "that allowing freezers in homes would make it too easy to plug televisions, radios, and all sorts of appliances into electrical outlets"[7]. The freezer was banned not because there was any danger of it individually breaking down Amish personal and community values, but because other worldly devices would likely piggy back off of it. Despite its ban, the Amish have adapted so that they can still benefit from the freezer. It's common for them to rent small storage freezers in fruit markets or stores or to own a freezer in a non-Amish neighbor's garage or basement. This arrangement helps the Amish with their goal of self-sufficiency while preventing other electrical devices from entering Amish homes.

According to Amish writer Elmo Stoll in *Strangers and Pilgrims: Why We Live Simply* there are four primary reasons why the Amish ban modern appliances in their quest to live simply.[8] First, the Amish take seriously the concept that they came into the world with nothing and will leave it with nothing. What purpose does it serve and what good comes from strolling through life feeling one must accumulate a plethora of material possessions, living a life revolving around them, and then dying without them having been deceived from one's real purpose in life? Living simply allows the Amish to avoid the temptation of placing their trust in material possessions and wasting their precious time pursuing these things.

Second, Stoll writes that a simple life is an expression of love for one's neighbor. Living in "luxury" places one in the position of being unfeeling and unresponsive toward the needs of others. Materialism makes a person overly sensitive to their own needs and desires rather than of those around them. A person who lives simply, absent all the unnecessary accoutrements of modern living, will find that their heart empathizes with the feelings of others in a like position to their own and those with even less. A greater sense of community develops because individuals feel a connectedness and relatedness to others.

Following the example set by Jesus serves as Stoll's third reason. Jesus lived simply and expected his disciples to live simply. He wanted his followers to trust Him to provide for their needs, which would help to increase their faith. Jesus taught about the dangers of loving the world and the things of the world. Living simply and placing one's trust in God are disciplines that grow stronger the more a believer practices them.

Finally, living simply is good for the character development of the children within a family. Children who are taught the value of work will live more pleasingly to God and will fare better in life. If appliances and other labor saving devices do all the work, then an opportunity is lost to teach important values to the child.

The Amish don't just live simply by avoiding modern conveniences. They also live simply in many other ways such as how they dress, how they furnish their home, how they worship, how they spend what free time they have, and how they conduct themselves in personal relationships. The term "plain" in describing the Amish goes hand-in-hand with "simple." The way the Amish live can accurately be described as plain and simple. There is nothing elaborate or showy about any aspect of Amish life, at least none that would be easy for non-Amish to see. The Amish try to live plainly so as not to draw undue attention to themselves as a result of pride. They emphasize the virtue of plainness, which is akin to humbleness, a spiritual value the Amish strive to exemplify in their lives.

Living simply is fully in line with Amish spiritual values and contributes to community adhesion and distinctiveness. To live any other way would expose the Amish to conveniences of modern life that would weaken spiritual commitment and tear the fabric of their community. Living simply requires personal sacrifice, but it's a sacrifice that the Amish are willing to make. Non-Amish can learn from the lessons expounded by Elmo Stoll about the benefits of simple living. While most non-Amish will likely never live as simply as the Amish do, they can nevertheless emulate some of these practices and generate anew a sense of spirituality vitality, family closeness, and community familiarity that are meaningful and fulfilling.

Do Not Lay Up for Yourselves Treasure on Earth

Living simply, for the Amish, is a matter of being faithful to scripture. The bible consistently teaches the importance of simple living and the avoidance of being captivated and dependent on earthly things. Physical possessions are to be used for the good they can provide us but are not to become objects of worship pulling us away from God. Simple and plain living is a discipline that continually reminds us in a positive way of our dependence on God and our humility before Him.

Simple and plain living serves as a barometer concerning our attitude towards wealth. In Matthew 6:19-21 it is written, *"Do not lay up for yourselves treasures on earth, where moth and rust destroy and where thieves break in and steal; but lay up for yourself treasures in heaven, where neither moth nor rust destroys and where thieves do not break in and steal. For where your treasure is, there your heart will be also."* Often, like the Pharisees of the bible, somewhere along the line we become intent on building up treasures here on earth. The exact reason we do this often depends on the particular person. We can do this for a sense of security, pride, love of soft living, projection of power, and to build up more wealth.

There is a saying in the substance abuse community that goes, "The man takes a drink, the drink takes a drink, and then the drink takes the man," describing a person's slide in alcoholism and loss of everything. Similarly, with our coveting of wealth and pretentious living we gradually slide into a dangerous, modern style of life that is far from the simplicity that God desires. The next verse of Matthew 6:22 states, *"The lamp of the body is the eye. If therefore your body is good, your whole body will be full of light. But if your eye is bad, your whole body will be full of darkness."* The Amish understand that today's materialism is a type of spiritual disease. Our spiritual eyes are diseased causing us to covet money and wealth ultimately leaving us in a spiritual darkness.

On the other hand, if we are occupied with the things of God, we will learn to live by faith, not by wealth and material possessions. Those possessions we have will be simple and utilitarian and not possessed to be a reflection of our inner pride. We will truly comprehend Jesus' words in Luke 12:22-24, *"Therefore I say to you, do not worry about your life, what you will eat; nor about your body, what you will put on. Life is more than food, and the body is more than clothing. Consider the ravens, for they neither sow nor reap, which have neither storehouse nor barn; and God feeds them. Of how much more value are you than the birds?"* Simple living is a reflection of our understanding concerning our value to God. When we seek to live in wealthy and materialistic ways this is a clear indicator that we don't understand how valuable we are to the Creator of the Universe. When we live simply, this shows on our part that we trust our lives to God and that we believe He values us.

The Amish see themselves as simply pilgrims passing through this life with no need to store up earthly treasures, and so should we as Christian believers. We, like the Amish, are to live our lives as strangers in a strange land dwelling here temporarily: *"By faith Abraham obeyed when he was called out to go to the place which he would receive as an inheritance. And he went out not knowing where he was going, By faith he dwelt in the land of promise as in a foreign country, dwelling in tents with Isaac and Jacob, the heirs with him of the same promise; for he waited for the city which has foundations, whose builder and maker is God"* (Hebrews 11:8-10). Pilgrims and strangers travel lightly as they seek their final destination. Our life as believers should resemble this simplicity of living.

In responding to an eager teacher of the law who wanted to follow him, Jesus noted that foxes have dens and birds have roosts but he maintained nowhere to lay down His head. To follow Christ is difficult no matter what, but it becomes nearly impossible if we attempt to encumber ourselves with worldly cares and possessions. The Amish are not hermits, casting off every physical possession and living in extreme isolation, but they do live plainly and simply in order to maintain their dependence and faith in God. In the final analysis, faith and dependence are excellent measuring instruments to gauge how simply we need to live.

Simple and Plain Living

To live simply and plainly in a similar spirit if not to the same degree as the Amish requires personal and spiritual introspection. The ability to measure ourselves against God's word is a great blessing in being able to make life changing adjustments to the way we are living. Many of the principles given below require personal and spiritual introspection in order to live more simply and plainly.

- *Adopt the right mindset for living simply and plainly.* When our mind is in agreement with our actions things go a lot more smoothly and successfully. In order to live more simply and plainly, it's very helpful to recognize and appreciate the positives in doing so. If our thoughts rebel against the concept of simple and plain living, and the knowledge of the potential benefits of this way of life cannot break through our steely determination against it, then it is best to not yet proceed. However, if the desire is there and the positive benefits seem to make good sense, then you are ready to begin to make changes. Elmo Stoll's four positives described earlier can be a good starting place, but you can also benefit by listing some ways simple and plain living will personally benefit you and your family.

- *Ask, "What in the way I live is hindering my relationship with God?"* By asking this question and taking time to examine all areas of your life you will undoubtedly start to identify practices and behaviors attributable to modern society that are hurting your relationship with God. Often these will revolve around materialism, pride, and seeking power and control. These are substitutes for a relationship with God and draw us further and further away from Him. Once you have identified these, depending on your personality, you may way to start eliminating the lesser ones first and then move on to the bigger ones. This way you build your confidence and experience in doing so. Simple and plain ways of living may naturally fall into place, but more than likely you will need to make an effort to deliberately choose such changes that you would like.

- *Focus more on the things of God.* Perhaps you have noticed like I have that those times when I get truly serious about being in God's Will and studying His Word I find the cares and desires of the world seem to affect me less and less. Jesus' words in Matthew 16:24-25 are helpful, *"Then Jesus said to his disciples, "If anyone desires to come after Me, let him deny himself, and take up his cross and follow Me. For whoever desires to save his life will lose it, but whoever loses his life for My sake will save it. For what profit is it it to a man if he gains the whole world, and loses his own soul?"* This comes directly after he told Peter, *"Get behind Me, Satan! You are an offense to Me, for you are not mindful of the things of God, but the things of men"* (Matthew 16:23). When you focus on the things of God this always means less of you and the things of the world. This translates as living more plainly and simply for God.

- *Periodically reevaluate your way of living.* In the world we live in and its fallen nature evil is constantly seeking to corrupt good unless preventative action is taken. Even the Amish struggle against creeping materialism and sin that threatens their way of life. By periodically evaluating your way of living you can better identify when you have gone off course and need a course correction. New products, styles, and habits are constantly being introduced into society and without realizing it you may adopt these along with their detrimental effects. Periodic reevaluations will help you to identify and delete these from your life.

Humility

The Amish place great value on the virtue of humility. Its essence is interwoven in the fabric of Amish consciousness and society. The Amish emphasis on humility is guided by passages from the bible such as Romans 12:16: *"Be of the same mind toward one another. Do not set your mind on high things, but associate with the humble. Do not be wise in your own opinion."* On the other hand the Amish are wary of the sin of pride and as a community will act to address it in a member who has come under its sway.

The 18th century Pietistic devotional "Rules for a Godly Life" containing proverbs on how to center one's daily life on God through thoughts, words, and deeds is popular with the Amish and touches frequently on humility. For example, one proverb says:

"If other people praise you, humble yourself. But do not praise yourself or boast, for that is the way of fools who seek vain praise. Be honest in all your dealings and this will be enough reward; then others will praise you."

Still another says:

Do not be proud and overbearing because you have been blessed with this world's goods, or with outstanding personality features; for God who has given can also take away, and may do so if through pride or contempt of others make misuse of His gifts to you. Even though you may possess certain qualities of which you may feel proud, they are more than offset by your many bad habits and shortcomings which prove you unworthy in your own eyes. He who knows himself well is certain to find enough of human frailty to make it extremely difficult for him to consider himself better than others."

In practice humility is expressed in various ways in the Amish community. One way is through deference to others or putting others first. Amish people seek to surrender their personal will to God's and submit to the authority of others within the community. They use the term *uffgeva,* meaning "giving up" describing the surrendering of their will to that of God and others.[9] As a result of this surrendering of will, the Amish defer to others and show reserve in their personal interactions. They will insist that others go before them and are cautious in their personal interactions so as not to seem excessively bold or attention seeking.

Another form of expressing humility is in the way the Amish dress. Amish dress, like modern society, communicates the values they hold to. Modern dress communicates individual preference, social class, and wealth. Humility is simply not part of the equation. Amish dress, on the other hand, communicates group membership and submission to the moral order.[10] Amish dress serves several functions including signaling the individual has yielded to the group, preventing dress from being used for self-adornment, promoting equality, and creating a common group identity.[11] The way of Amish dress is a statement to the world and each other of their humility and yielding to the supremacy of the group.

The Amish express humility in their material possessions as well. Material possessions communicate a lot about a person and often are specifically designed to do so. In modern society material possessions are designed to communicate wealth, exclusiveness, power, freedom, sophistication, and class. Very rarely are modern material possessions designed with humility in mind. Amish material possessions communicate the opposite and the Amish seek to have fewer possessions, which they hold to very lightly. The possessions of the Amish are plain and simple and communicate a sense of humbleness that the Amish value. Those Amish who are tempted to show off and brag about their wealth and possessions are charged with pride and arrogance and required to change their way of living.[12]

The Amish take seriously the personal struggle of humility verses pride. Pride entices them away from God while humility draws them back. In order to remain close to God the Amish have made deliberate choices to promote humility in areas such as personal appearance, possessions, language, and deference to others. Like all people, the Amish experience pride as an ever present temptation and like all people they sometimes succumb to it. However, the personal and communal decisions made by the Amish to limit pride and promote humility have served them effectively for centuries.

Grace to the Humble

Humility begins first in our relationship with God. It is realized in our life when we come to the point when we truly recognize our status before God. We are one of His creatures meaning that He has the power to create us as well as the power to destroy us if He so desires. But He doesn't desire this because He loves us so much. The way a parent loves a child is faint in comparison to the way God loves us. His love, however, does not permit us to equate ourselves with Him in any way. He desires an attitude of lowliness and obedience from us. God exalts those who are humble and disciplines those who are proud as seen throughout scriptures in verses like Proverbs 3:34: *"Surely he scorns the scornful, but gives grace to the humble,"* and Luke 1:52, *"He has put down the mighty from their thrones, and exalted the lowly."*

God does not leave the choice of humility up to us but commands it. For example, Micah 6:8 records, *"He has shown you, O man, what is good; And what does the Lord require of you but to do justly, to love mercy, and to walk humbly with your God?"* Have you ever had extended dealings with someone who is arrogant and prideful? Do you remember how difficult that person could be? This type of person is inconsiderate of the feelings of others, think they know what is right every time, and think they are better than others. Like the warning in Proverbs 16:18, *"Pride goes before destruction, and a haughty spirit before a fall,"* prideful people often bring trouble to themselves and those around them. God desires what is best for us because of His great love and pride is not one of those things. When we direct our child not to do something dangerous, like playing in the street, this is similar to God commanding us to be humble and not prideful. It is what is good for us and others.

God not doesn't just command us to be humble but exalts us for doing so. Remember David's position before he became king. He was a shepherd following the sheep all day long. Partly or mainly because of his humility and obedience to God, he was taken from the sheep and made ruler over Israel. And is there anyone more humble in spirit and in action in the bible, other than Christ, than John the Baptist? Scripture says he dressed, lived and ate humbly and was obedient to the Lord: *"Now John himself was clothed in camel's hair, with a leather belt around his waist; and his food was locusts and wild honey"* (Matthew 3:4). In reward for his humbleness and obedience John's exaltation is unimaginable—he was allowed to baptize God Himself (Matthew 3:13-17).

There is a funny but true saying that it's hard to be humble. The average Christian believer struggles with the temptation of pride just like anyone else. However, the believer typically has an inkling that pride is wrong and humility is right, while the unbeliever may not. Christians struggle with the temptation of pride because they too often allow themselves to be drawn too close too frequently by the allure of its brightly illuminating flame. And then, of course, they are burned by it. The Amish on the other hand, while also tempted by pride, are less frequently burned by it because individually and societally they have made it a point to keep themselves further away. Pride is much more socially unacceptable among the Amish than regular society. Non-Amish Christians, on the other hand, tend to be fence straddlers between pride and humility. It's hard to be humble when *both* feet are not firmly grounded in humility.

The beginning of humbleness starts with repentance. Humbleness is a spiritual attitude and way of life that requires repentance from the pride that has pervaded our lives. Second Kings 22:19 illustrates a time of repentance and humbleness before God by King Josiah, *"'...because your heart was tender, and you humbled yourself before the Lord when you heard what I spoke against this place and against its inhabitants, that they would become a desolation and a curse, and you tore your clothes and wept before Me, I also have heard you', says the Lord."* Humbleness requires a tenderness of heart that is willing and able to receive the impressions of God. A hardened heart is one that has been so calloused by the pride and haughtiness of the world that it is impervious to God. A tender heart will receive God's impressions and as a result act in the way in which God wants it too—in the case of pride it will cause the person to act by seeking repentance.

Once we have sought repentance, the bible offers no better teacher of humility than Christ Himself. Philippians 2:5-8 describes in a nutshell the glorious humility exemplified in the life of Christ: *"Let this mind be in you that was also in Christ Jesus, who, being in the form of God, did not consider it robbery to be equal with God, but made himself of no reputation, taking the form of a bondservant, and coming in the likeness of men. And being found in appearance as a man, He humbled himself and became obedient to the point of death, even the death of the cross."* Try to imagine what it must have been like to be

Creator of the universe and then to willingly give it all up to live in a world in which life is short, brutish and nasty—and you were to be the primary object of such brutishness and nastiness. Hopefully, this helps you better understand what becoming humble means as you reflect on Jesus' submission to the Father's will.

Humble Living

Living humbly requires the right spiritual orientation. A person can be a believer and not necessarily be humble. Just take a look at many of the professed Christians in the public eye and how their actions are often self-promoting and proud. Lesser known Christians, like you and me, also often struggle with pride. For the believer, living in a humble manner is as difficult a goal as any other spiritual pursuit. Here are some suggestions on living humbly that I hope will help.

- *Start with repentance.* As I have grown older I've looked back on my past attitudes and actions and can only shake my head at how prideful I could be at times. Humility was more often than not, not in the equation. The young are not the only ones to struggle with pride though. No matter what age pride is a constant temptation. When I've thought back I've felt a sense of regret for my pride and at different times have asked God for forgiveness. I'm never out of the woods when it comes to pride but sincerely repenting of it is the right start. Repentance helps to flush out the old attitudes and behaviors holding you back and prepares you for a fresh start.

- *Give up your will to God and others.* As mentioned previously, the Amish practice *uffgeva* or the surrendering of their will to God and the community. At the core of humility is being willing to place God and others before yourself. Naturally, in our individualistic society some who read this may think this borders on scandalous. Self, self, self has been so drilled into us that putting God and others before our self is almost unthinkable. If you think in such a way you need not worry. Human nature is such that we will almost always love our self more than others and give ourselves plenty of attention. The real danger is not in neglecting self it is in neglecting God and others. Surrendering our will to God is part of the brokenness that is associated with repentance. When we realize we can no longer live this life on our own and we need God's guiding hand, we then are open to giving up our will to His. And when we are willing to surrender our will to His we are then more open to giving up our wants and desires in favor of others. Learning to give up your will to God and others takes time so be patient with yourself.

- *Know yourself well.* When you glance at yourself in the mirror from a distance you might think "Not too bad." However, when you get really close up to the mirror and start to examine yourself minutely then you may begin to notice spots and blemishes that aren't so sightly. Being humble as a Christian is aided when we have examined and know ourself well. When we do so we come to recognize the imperfections of spirit and character that are part of who we are. Awareness of these will help to adjust our attitude to one of greater humility and our dependence upon God. We better see how far we are from God's will and how weak and powerless we are on our own. When we reach the point that we continually acknowledge our need for God and

His strength we will find a greater willingness to humble ourselves before Him.

- *Recognize how truly wonderful others are as God's creation.* How often do we consider someone and immediately all their many flaws come to mind? It's almost like we have a need to belittle others in our mind in order to make ourselves feel better about who we are. In doing so we miss an opportunity to grow spiritually by exalting others before ourself. Each of us is fearfully and wonderfully made by the Creator. When we can recognize how unique and beautiful each person is as a reflection of God Himself, rather than tearing them down in our heart, we will then be more willing to humble ourselves and lift others up. We will be less inclined to boast about who we are and more willing to cherish the special qualities of others. Recently, I was watching the Olympic Games in London on television. One track runner who had just smashed the world record in the 100m and was being praised by so many, still couldn't help himself proudly self-proclaiming how he thought he was the "greatest" Olympian of all time and how he had "no respect" for a previous well known gold medal Olympian in the same sport. At what should have been time of triumph and humility he revealed the true nature of his heart by the pride and contempt he held for his fellow man.

Family

The Amish have perhaps the strongest and most stable family system in America. Divorce is almost unheard of, families are large, and bonds are close between family members. The reason for this strength and stability rests on the preeminent importance family and parenting are given by the Amish. Every decision the Amish make personally and corporately is made with the best interests of the family in mind.

Amish families have a number of unique characteristics that distinguish them from other American households and contribute to their strength. One of these is the great emphasis the Amish place on the value of the family. Whenever a decision has to be made the Amish question what effect it will have on the family. If the decision means the weakening of the family, the Amish will reject such a choice. For this reason many of the activities that modern American families participate in the Amish abstain from. They understand that these activities, such as television viewing and internet surfing, will only create distance between family members and between families.

Working and being together is a vital component of Amish families. Traditionally, the Amish have maintained family farms keeping them close to home and constantly in touch with their loved ones. A decrease in available land and a sharp spike in prices have caused many to go to work in factories, shops and businesses. While this has made it more difficult to be together, the Amish still emphasize that whatever available time they have they will spend with one another as family.

The Amish also maintain traditional family roles. Amish husbands and wives have distinct gender roles that modern couples are increasingly finding blurred. Amish men and women appreciate such differences and are raised to understand the value of them. While no relationship is perfect, not even among the Amish, they do not experience the artificially generated battle between the sexes that is so prevalent in modern society. More will be said about the role of children momentarily, but in brief they are taught from a very young age to be meek, humble, and obedient and to show respect for their elders.

The elderly among the Amish are respected and valued. They are not shipped off to retirement homes in their old age. They continue to live near or with their children while helping with family responsibilities and helping to raise and guide their grandchildren. The lessons they teach their children and grandchildren are helpful in shaping character and maintaining the Amish way of life. The Amish also maintain close relationships with their extended family and are actively involved in one another's lives. Aunts, uncles, cousins and others maintain close personal relationships and are mutually supportive.

The Amish place great value and invest much time in their children. Every child is a welcomed addition and is given much love and attention. The average Amish family is large compared to modern standards with 6-7 children on average. These children are raised and actively taught the Amish way. Discipline is heavily emphasized in Amish families. Starting around age two Amish children are taught respect, obedience and responsibility. Light corporal punishment is sometimes used but is not always necessary.

Amish children are taught about God every step of the way. Amish parents do not leave the teaching about God to others. They take an active role in helping the child to understand and be obedient to God's will. Whatever facet of life they are involved in Amish children are shown how God plays an important part. Unlike American public schools, in Amish schools God is emphasized and whether through songs, scripture reading or in academic lessons God is plainly evident.

The value and importance of work is taught to Amish children as well. From the youngest age Amish children are given work to do and are made to feel valuable for what they contribute. As they age they are given greater responsibilities preparing them for life ahead. Children go to school until the eighth grade at which time they are then expected to begin working full-time on the farm or business contributing to the welfare of the family. The fruits of their labor is considered to belong to the family until such time as they are ready to leave the home and start a family of their own. An Amish child grows up with a strong work ethic which they then in turn pass on to their own children.

Amish children are also taught the values of sharing and helping others. By observing the example of their parents they learn that it is truly better to give than receive. The Amish are typically generous with their material possessions, money, and provisions. Not only do they give, but they help others as well. When another family is in need of assistance the Amish will give of their time and labor, even if it means their own needs go wanting. The children of the Amish observe this giving and helping attitude and adopt it as their own. They are also directly taught it from scripture, stories and personal guidance.

At one time in the life of America, Amish families and those of the rest of the country didn't used to be so different. But as time passed and secular society changed the differences between Amish and non-Amish widened. Amish families retained most of their cherished values that promote the health and strength of the family, while much of the rest of society traded theirs in for weaker relativistic values. The harmful results are plainly evident when one compares the weakened structure and functioning of the average modern American family compared to the Amish.

Be Fruitful and Multiply

The Amish base their experience of family and parenting on scripture. They use scripture as a regular reminder of the value and importance of marriage and children and the roles they're to take. And in fact, from the very beginning of scripture, guidance is provided as to the role of men and women in relation to their union and purpose. For example, Genesis 1:27-28 describes the initial beginnings of the marital relationship and God's directions to the first couple: "*So God created man in His own image; in the image of God He created him; male and female He created them. Then God blessed them, and God said to them, 'Be fruitful and multiply; fill the earth and subdue it...'*" Marriage has several purposes as seen in this scripture and others. Man and woman come from creation itself and so are of the same substance and are designed to be dependent upon one another. Marriage is a means for companionship and is meant to be a committed, exclusive relationship (Gen.

2:18; Gen. 2:23-24; Mark 10:7-8). Marriage is designed to be a lifelong partnership (Matt. 19:6) in which children are raised (Mal. 2:15). Amish marriages are not perfect and couples struggle with relationship issues just like modern couples. The difference is that the Amish are taught to understand the deeper purpose for marriage, to be committed to the marriage despite their problems, and to work to make it better.

Once married, Amish couples easily take on the traditional marital role they have been trained for their whole life. Some of this training is through instruction such as during a sermon, but most is learned from observing their parents and other couples and from practicing these roles before they are married. Scripture is also a primary source the Amish use to define their roles in marriage and family. Ephesians 5:22-31 is a definitive passage of scripture for the Amish and is worth repeating in sum here:

"Wives, submit to your own husbands, as to the Lord. For the husband is head of the wife, as also Christ is head of the church; and He is the Savior of the body. Therefore, just as the church is subject to Christ, so let the wives be to their own husbands in everything. Husbands, love your wives, just as Christ also loved the church and gave Himself for her, that He might sanctify and cleanse her with the washing of water by the word, that He might present her to Himself a glorious church, not having spot or wrinkle or any such thing, but that she should be holy and without blemish. So husbands ought to love their own wives as their own bodies; he who loves his wife loves himself. For no one ever hated his own flesh, but nourishes and cherishes it, just as the Lord does the church. For we are members of His body, of His flesh and of His bones. 'For this reason a man shall leave his father and mother and

be joined to his wife, and the two shall become one flesh.'"

God is head over all things and Jesus is head over all creation. It stands to reason that within creation God delegates authority to one head of the family—the husband. Amish wives recognize the headship of the husband, and the husband is responsible to treat his wife and children with love and kindness. While Amish couples often confer over issues and problems facing the family, the husband ultimately has the decision making authority. To have both husband and wife with equal authority would lead to confusion and conflict. One bible scholar has said *"Fifty-fifty marriages are an impossibility. They do not work. They cannot work. In marriage someone has to be the final decision maker. Someone has to delegate responsibility, and God has ordained that this should be the husband."* Most Amish see it this way too.

Children are thought of by the Amish as a gift from God, and so they are eagerly anticipated and welcomed. Scripture such as Psalm 127:3, *"Behold, children are a heritage from the Lord, the fruit of the womb is a reward,"* and Genesis 33:5, *"And he lifted his eyes and saw the women and children, and said, 'Who are these with you?' So he said 'The children whom God has graciously given your servant,'"* confirm in the mind of the Amish the wonderful blessing that children are meant to be. Despite how wonderful children are, however, they are also thought of as being lost spiritually and immature in their understanding of Christ. It is the parent's and community's responsibility to raise their children up in knowledge and understanding of the Lord. Amish parents take this role very seriously and usually devote a tremendous amount of time teaching their children the precepts of God's word and how to live this out in daily life. Fathers and mothers feel responsible to love, discipline and instruct their children (Psalms 103:13; Prov. 13:24; Psalms 78:2-8).

In turn, children are expected to honor their mother and father (Exodus 20:12). Amish fathers and mothers also expect their children to obey them and heed their guidance (Col. 3:20; Prov. 23:22). When Amish children disobey their parent's discipline is quickly utilized, though the Amish seek to avoid disciplining in anger. The Amish are mindful of the benefits of discipline and are wary of the consequences of not disciplining. Hebrews 12:7-11 helps to guide their thinking:

"If you endure chastening, God deals with you as with sons; for what son is there whom a father does not chasten? But if you are without chastening, of which all have become partakers, then you are illegitimate and not sons. Furthermore, we have had human fathers who corrected us, and we paid them respect. Shall we not much more readily be in

subjection to the Father of spirits and live? For they indeed for a few days chastened us as seemed best to them, but He for our profit, that we may be partakers of His holiness. Now no chastening seems to be joyful for the present, but painful; nevertheless, afterward it yields the peaceable fruit of righteousness to those who have been trained by it."

Without question the Amish take their roles as husband and wife and as parents seriously, using scripture as a primary guide in their endeavors. Despite their seriousness, love for one another pervades much of their life. Scripture serves as a primary tool of instruction and they turn to it daily in such matters.

Building Family

Non-Amish can follow the example of the Amish in a number of ways to strengthen their family and help in their parenting. As previously mentioned, Amish marital relationships have issues just like modern couples do but their deep sense of commitment to the marriage helps them to work through these. They also struggle at times with parenting issues, but because they take parenting seriously from the very earliest stages of a child's life the issues that arise are typically of less consequential nature than moderns. If you are willing to make some basic changes in your marital and parenting relationships it is possible for you to realize some of the same benefits the Amish do.

- *Make God first and family second in your life.* This guidance seems commonsensical, and it is. But if you look at your life right now is this the way it is arranged in actual practice? If many of us examine how things actually are ordered in our lives it is often job first, family second, and God somewhere a distant third, fourth or fifth. The strength of the Amish way of life is that by placing God first in all things the family reaps the fruit of their commitment. Since God is a God of love, and He wants us to love our family and others, then by placing Him first we are more likely to love our family in a similar way to how He loves us. Even if we place family first in our life we are doing them a disservice because we are not teaching them that God is preeminent. We are teaching our loved ones that self is more important than God and this is a form of pride that will harm our family relations in the long run.

- *Follow Godly principles and teach Godly principles.* Nothing is more important to the Amish than passing on their knowledge and love of God to the next generation. Amish fathers and mothers continually seek opportunities to help one another grow in Christ and to enlighten their children about Christian beliefs. Most teaching is accomplished through leading by example. An Amish mother or father is acutely aware of the message their words and actions relay to their children, so they do their best to set the right example. They don't always succeed but they cannot be faulted for not putting forth the effort. If you want to have a stronger more Christ focused family then lead by example in following Godly principles, encourage your family to do so as well, and look for everyday opportunities to teach about the Lord.

- *Take an accounting of where your family currently stands and make appropriate changes.* Maybe you are reading this because you sense your family is not where it should be spiritually and relationally. Take stock of where your family is and where you think the Lord wants it to be. What is your family doing well and you would like to maintain? What things are not so good and causing you concern? What things are spiritually harming your family and what things are helping? The answers to these questions will help you decide what needs to change for the better and what needs to stay as is. It can be difficult to change family patterns and reject familiar activities so you will have prepare your family for the changes it needs to make. Spending more time together, for example, may mean limiting or eliminating other activities. Growing spiritually closer and more active as a family will necessitate adding more spiritual activities. At first, family members may not be as excited about it as you are, but if you lead by example and help them experience the blessings they will eventually follow your lead.

- *Make being together a priority.* A happy, healthy family needs time together. There is no replacement for spending time with one another. Quality time does not equal quantity time, and in fact quality time is a direct result of having enough quantity time. Every family has responsibilities and interests. Responsibilities are those activities you involve yourself in that you must do to keep the family functioning. Interests are those things that you do that you or your family members have a personal interest in but are not absolutely essential. Too often families spend little time together because they are so wrapped up in their personal responsibilities (such as work) or interests (such as hobbies). To spend more time together something has to change. Obviously interests are the first place to start. To make more time for family you can either eliminate certain personal interests or you can refocus your personal interests to become family interests. Instead of doing things by yourself do them together as a family. Sometimes, however, responsibilities need to change. This isn't always as easy as our responsibilities often financially support our family. If this is the case, but you still want to make more time for your family, you can ask those for whom you work for a change of your schedule or you can change responsibilities, such as changing jobs. You may balk saying this is unreasonable, but if you take the Amish as an example, there are many instances where an Amish father has given up or changed jobs in order to be with family more. Sure, there may have been a cut in pay or a starting over, but this is the sacrifice most Amish are willing to make for their family. How about you?

- *Give your children responsibilities and teach them the importance of sharing with and helping others.* These three cornerstones of Amish parenting will be just as valuable for your children as they are for the Amish. A child that is given household responsibilities will feel valued and competent and will learn an early work ethic that will benefit them as they go forward in life. A child that is taught to share with and help others will continue these practices as lifelong behaviors that will help to build relationships and love for others. Not having these expectations of your children will increase the chance of the child growing up to be irresponsible and selfish.

Spirituality

Unlike many modern Christians the Amish do not separate their spiritual life from their daily life. They do not reserve Christian practice and worship to just Sundays. Their spirituality is interwoven into the everyday fabric of their life. Modern believers have unwittingly consumed the secular dogma that faith must be separated from daily life. When believers choose to go along with the separation of their faith from other aspects of their life the proverbial pie is then cut in such a way as to heavily favor the world. As time goes on the unsuspecting believer finds that the world is winning the battle to consume the ever shrinking slice of faith in his or her life.

The Amish reject this artificial separation of spiritual faith and daily life. They believe that spiritual faith and spiritual practice are inseparably intertwined with one another and everyday life. Amish faith is holistic and the

Amish resist breaking down and separating life into its component parts.

One advantage of maintaining an integrated whole when it comes to spirituality is that the Amish see every day and every moment as an opportunity to publicly witness through their actions. Unlike evangelicals who emphasize using words to share the gospel with others, the Amish stress the importance of actions as a primary form of witness. The Amish believe the best way to judge a person's faith is to see it lived in context, in community.[13] "Letting your light shine" is stressed throughout the Amish community meaning allowing others to see their faith and good works as a way to point them to Jesus.

Along with interweaving faith and daily life the Amish also practice other aspects of Christian spirituality in unique ways compared to modern Christians. Amish prayer life is anchored in rich tradition and is actively practiced. The Amish hold on to traditional prayer practices by praying from centuries old texts reflecting the experiences and prayer needs of their forefathers. At the same time, they also encourage individual private prayer among family members. While Amish prayer may seem more formalized and structured than modern prayers, it's typically also practiced more regularly and intently. Fasting, or going without food for a certain period of time, often accompanies Amish prayer as well. The Amish also read devotional texts of various kinds including those read by modern Christians such as *Our Daily Bread* and Oswald Chamber's *My Utmost for His Highest.*[14]

Sundays are a day of worship, rest, and reverence for the Amish. Many of the practices that early Americans traditionally followed on Sundays but have since abandoned the Amish still abide by. For example, the Amish cease to work on Sundays other than preparing meals and caring for animals. They also avoid traveling for activities that could be handled on any other day. Sunday is reserved for worship and rest. The Amish attend church services every other week. On off Sundays they may attend a church service at a different church than their own, or they may just use the day to rest and focus on family and God. In doing so they may read scripture together, spend time in a quite devotion, visit friends, shut-ins or families with new babies. Such activities help to build the strength of the local community.

When they worship the Amish emphasize unity in spirit and practice. While their preachers deliver individual sermons everything else that happens in worship is done collectively, whether prayer or singing. Singing solos, choirs, and musical performances are considered "showy display" and are not part of Amish worship.[15] Even prayers are practiced collectively and it would be rare for an individual to offer a prayer out loud. Spoken words in worship emphasize humility and submission and the congregation is encouraged to be more humble and submissive in their daily life. Similarly, the Amish avoid using terms such as "assurance of salvation" as many evangelicals do. The Amish feel to claim such would be presumptuous, since in their belief salvation is a judgment that only God can make at the end of one's life.[16]

The Amish also believe maintaining the church's purity is of great importance. As a result, they have procedures in place to address wayward members. They continue to follow the direction of the Dordrecht Confession of Faith from the 17th Century. The Confession states in regards to church purity, "An offensive member and open sinner [must] be excluded from the church, rebuked before all and purged out as leaven and thus remain until his amendment, as an example and warning to others and also that the church may be kept pure from such 'spots' and blemishes."[17] As a result, order, authority, and identity take precedence over tolerance.[18] Those Amish who are unwilling to change their ways after having been warned can be banned from the community until they repent and alter their ways.

Spiritually, the Amish recognize that they live in a "dualistic world" in which they are "a Christian community suspended in a tension field between obedience to God and those who have rejected Go in their disobedience. Purity and goodness are in conflict with impurity and evil."[19] As such, they recognize that their spiritual vitality comes at a price.[20] The Amish place great spiritual and other demands on themselves, but believe the reward of a pure and vibrant faith is worth the cost. They also take seriously those spiritual perils that detract from their sacred duty and purpose. Addressing these requires "time, effort, and intentionality," which they are willing to offer up.[21]

Let Your Light So Shine

The Amish faith is a lived out faith. By this I mean great emphasis is placed on living in such a way that others are influenced positively for Christ. The words of Christ in Matthew 5:16 bear special meaning for the Amish who try to faithfully follow his admonition, *"Let your light so shine before men, that they may see your good works and glorify your father in heaven."*

Too often modern Christians have fallen in the practice of "checking their faith at the door." This is not what the Lord intended. God wants us to bring our faith into the world; into our workplace; into our home. Our mission is to become the salt of the earth so that we cannot only experience the presence of Christ in our lives, but also bring Him into the lives of others. Checking our faith at the door is a serious error in which we overly accommodate the beliefs and sensitivities of everyone else but neglect our own. First John 2:6 tells us that those who abide in Christ ought to walk just as He walked. We are not going to be able to walk like Christ if our faith is not part of that walk no matter where we are.

Living out our faith and letting our light shine does not mean an "in your face" kind of activity. Philippians 2:12 tells us to continue to *"work out your own salvation with fear and trembling..."* "Fear and trembling" here is best summarized as living out our faith with humility. Humility in the sense that no good work is truly our work, but rather it is God's and we should not be boastful. Humility also in the sense that we should be respectful and understanding of others and that we convey this to them so that they should take an interest in learning what makes us as we are, which is Christ. Working out our salvation in this verse means living out the faith we have in Christ. Similar to Philippians 1:27 we should be conducting ourselves in a manner worthy of the gospel.

One of the ways the Amish live out their faith and let their light shine is by keeping the holy things of God holy. Take the keeping of the Sabbath, for example. Most non-believers recognize that the Sabbath, normally on Sunday in America, is a special day, a holy day, even if they don't observe it themselves. They might even be aware of scripture that says, *"And on the seventh day God ended His work which He had done, and he rested on the seventh day from all His work which He had done. Then God blessed the seventh day and sanctified it, because in it He rested from all His work which God had created and made"* (Genesis 2:2-3). Such a non-believer or even half-hearted believer is likely going to respect a Christian who takes God's word seriously and attempts to keep the Sabbath holy. The Amish, who set aside their work and use the day to focus on God, will influence others positively for Christ by the example they set. Other believers who treat the day just like any other day are going to have a negative influence or no influence at all on the unbeliever.

Not only are the Amish to be commended for keeping God's command to keep the Sabbath holy, but they also accrue other benefits meant to be received by

God as a result of keeping the Sabbath holy. For example, they will experience the refreshment and rejuvenating of the minds and bodies by resting (Exodus 31:17). They place themselves closer to God, which will allow them to fully receive His revelations (Revelation 1:10-11). The will be blessed by God (Isaiah 56:2). They will receive fruitfulness and prosperity (Isaiah 58:13-14) and so on.

Unity is another aspect of spirituality of vital importance to the Amish that other believers can learn from. The importance of unity to the Amish is based on scriptural teaching as well as the Amish desire to maintain close communal bonds. Scripturally, Philippians 2:1-3 serves as a guide, *"If you have any encouragement from being united with Christ, if any comfort from his love, if any fellowship with the Spirit, if any tenderness and compassion, then make my joy complete by being like-minded, having the same love, being one in spirit and purpose. Do nothing out of selfish ambition or vain conceit, but in humility consider others better than yourselves."* The blessings of such unity are found in verse two and include being like-minded, having the same love, and being one in spirit and purpose. Modern Christians in their daily exposure to secular influences are constantly taught the opposite of unity such as conflict is good, putting self first, and harboring feelings of hate and resentment toward others. Turn on almost any television show and you will find these attitudes glorified. It is no wonder that conflict is often the norm of many modern churches.

Similar to unity, maintaining spiritual purity is in itself challenging as well. It's challenging at the personal level and even more so at the church body level. Many modern churches have de-emphasized maintaining church purity and have given up any form of discipline for wayward church members. In order for something to become pure, however, the impure must be removed from it. As Ephesians 5:3 states in regard to separating the impure from the pure, *"But among you there must not be even a hint of sexual immorality, or of any kind of impurity, or of greed, because these are improper for God's holy people,"* impurity must not co-exist with purity. Discipline within the church serves the good purpose of achieving purity. Without discipline the church loses its ability to function as a part of Christ's body. Hebrews 12:10-11 sums this up stating *"For they indeed for a few days chastened us as seemed best to them, but He for our profit, □that we may be partakers of His holiness. □Now no □chastening seems to be joyful for the present, but painful; nevertheless, afterward it yields □the peaceable fruit of righteousness to those who have been trained by it."* The Amish continue to recognize that the benefit of discipline within the body of believers is greater purity. Modern bodies of believers would do well to recognize this benefit as well.

Vibrant Spirituality

Achieving and maintaining a vibrant spirituality requires commitment and effort on the part of the believer. It does not come without a cost. The Amish recognize that in order to maintain their faith and way of life there is a price to pay. Achieving and maintaining a vibrant spirituality is a blessing that God wants every believer to experience. The following suggestions are designed to help you have this blessing.

- *Integrate your spiritual life with every other aspect of your life.* As I wrote previously, modern believers have swallowed the dogma that they should separate their spirituality from the rest of their life, particularly that part of their life that interacts publicly. The reason for this insistence on separation of faith and daily life is so that your faith will not be an influence on non-believers. Is this what scripture says you should do? Are you to have only a private faith that is obscure to others? No, of course not. Whether you are one who feels led to verbally share your Christian faith with others or you allow your actions to do most of the talking you are to let your light to shine. If you have a disconnected faith you need to start the process of re-integrating your faith with the rest of your being. This will require intentionality on your part and a steady focus on bringing together what you believe with you who actually are. Do not shrink from allowing others to see that you are a Christian believer with specific beliefs and values.

- *Increase those habits that grow you spirituality.* A vibrant spirituality is dependent on what you feed it. The more it is fed with the right spiritual nourishment the more vibrant it will be. If you have ever fed fertilizer to a growing vegetable you know what a significant difference it can make to the health and production of that plant. Your spiritual health is dependent upon what you do on a daily basis to nourish it. Prayer, study of the bible, worship, devotions, giving, fellowship and other such Christian activities serve as rich soil for your spiritual growth. You will begin to notice significant improvement in your spiritual vitality the more you involve yourself in these Christian habits.

- *Seek to strengthen your relationship and unity with other believers.* As mentioned previously, the Amish place great emphasis on unity within the community. They spend significant amounts of time visiting, worshipping and fellowshipping with one another. In contrast, many modern believers, like the rest of culture, have retreated into their homes to worship at the altar of their televisions or computers rarely seen by other church members or neighbors. This is part hyperbole but part truth as well. Even when in the presence of fellow believers much time is spent thumbing on their smart phones as if the others really aren't there. Unity in Christ isn't built this way, but disunity is. In order to strengthen your relationship and unity with other believers you must spend time with them in order to know them better and walk with them through their troubles and good times.

- *Seek personal purity and fellowship with a body of believers who expect purity as well.* At the core of Christian spirituality is the necessity of purity. Christianity calls each of us to a higher and purer way of life. Without the continual quest for purity as a Christian your spiritual life will suffer. To become pure means to expel from yourself those things which are impure while bringing in those which are not. Modern believers often are unaware of how the impurities of the world have penetrated their daily life. We often minimize or rationalize those activities and behaviors that cause impurity because we don't see them as such. We see them as harmless fun, but in reality they are a corrosive influence on our spirituality. Even when other believers become aware of the impurities in our life and our obviously sinful behavior, they often say nothing about it to us, either because they too have the same impurities or because they think it is not their responsibility to do so. Our need is to take an honest accounting of our lives with the Word of God as our standard. We may even need the assessment of others. Once we recognize what impurities exist and in what form they take then we need to begin the process of purging them from our lives. We will also want to be part of a body of believers who value purity for they will help to hold us accountable and to keep the community in which we worship pure.

- *Evaluate your spiritual life as to whether you are paying a spiritual price or not.* Spirituality vitality comes at a price. You will be required to give up cherished relationships, possessions, and activities as well as endure hardships in order to experience a thriving spirituality. You will notice that your spiritual life is costing you something. Examine your life and determine whether your spirituality is costing you anything. If it is not, then it's quite possible that spiritually you have come to a standstill. You will want to make changes to your life so that you are actively pursuing spiritual growth, which will then come at a cost. Every day the Amish do without the conveniences and entertainment of modern culture because they want to maintain a vibrant spirituality. They have also even stood up against governing authorities when necessary to preserve their Christian beliefs and practices. They spend time concerning themselves with the things of God so that their spirituality will be nourished.

Community

The Amish way of community is significantly different from the society which surrounds it. Two related attitudes characterize and define the Amish way of community. The first is that of *uffgevva* which means "giving up" or the surrendering of selfish interests and desires. Giving up requires "yielding one's personal will to God's will, submitting to the authority of others within the community (parents, teachers, church leaders), and submitting to the wisdom of the group."[22] The second is *gelassenheit* and similar to *uffgevva* means "yieldedness or submission" to God's will and that of the community. These two attitudes and the ways in which they are lived out among the Amish distinguish these believers from the individualistic, self-interested society encircling them.

The Amish seek to lose self to the will of God and the community. Giving up and yielding shapes their religious convictions and habits. For example, worship is much more of a community activity than is typical for modern believers. When the Amish worship, they don't do so in a church building but gather together as a local community in the home of one of the members. Great efforts are made before hand to prepare the home for the worshippers, which can exceed 200 people. Family members arrive early on Sunday to help with last minute preparations and the first worshippers begin arriving around 8:00 A.M.in their buggies. Worship begins at around 9:00 A.M. and continues on for several hours. Afterwards, a light meal is served while members visit with one another before heading home. Teens will get together to spend time with one another later the same say. Two weeks later, the same local community of worshippers will gather at another member's home and follow the same procedure. The point here is that worship is truly a community event in which members of the local district are deeply involved in the daily life of one another.

Visiting among the Amish has been described as the "national sport" and the "social glue that bonds the community together through informal ties of trust and respect."[23] Off Sundays, or the Sundays when a particular Amish district doesn't hold worship services, is a favorite time for Amish families to visit with one another. Customarily, a visiting Amish family will arrive at the friend's house just before noon. Several families may already have arrived for visiting. The men handle the horses and buggies while the women prepare the tables for dinner. Some will gather in a sitting room in a circle until the women call everyone together for the meal. The afternoon is spent talking in the living room where the men are joined by the women after the dishes are done. In late afternoon, the children are gathered and the families head home. Other forms of visiting include visiting relatives unannounced, visiting the sick after worship service, and receiving visitors from out of state.[24] Such visiting patterns strengthen the bonds of community among the Amish as well as yielding to the interests of the community.

The Amish community is also small scale and largely self-sufficient. By small scale it is meant that wherever the Amish live the church district is the governing body and the church district is usually composed of thirty to forty households. These households form a congregation. The size of the congregation is limited by the distance members can reasonably travel by horse-and-carriage. Should a congregation grow greater than thirty to forty households a new congregation would need to form. The smallness in size of a congregation adds to the sense of community between members and allows them to have relatively intimate relationships with one another. While Amish communities are highly-integrated, they are not totally self-sufficient.[25] They still must rely on local markets, merchants, hospitals and medical services. However, they do strive for self-sufficiency as much as possible and are able to provide for their own socialization, religious and educational needs. They also provide much of their own food and take care of many of their own physical needs. Mutual aid among the Amish also assists in meeting the community's needs. The smallness of scale and striving for self-sufficiency enhance the Amish sense of closeness and community to a much greater degree than the non-Amish experience.

Another aspect of Amish life that contributes to strong communal bonds is their willingness to follow collective regulations, prohibitions, and expectations, which together is known as the *Ordnung*. *Ordnung* means "order" but more broadly refers to "the accumulated wisdom, the corporate guidelines that specify expectations for members."[26] The *Ordnung* is ratified by members twice a year and members are expected to follow the guidelines as much as possible. The *Ordnung* generally seeks to apply biblical principles of humility, obedience, and nonresistance to everyday issues not addressed by the Bible.[27] The *Ordnung* serves to place all the Amish in a particular district on the same page enabling the community to function as harmoniously as possible.

The Amish make intentional decisions designed to strengthen and enhance the communal bond of the congregants. These decisions are often foreign to the surrounding society and sometimes in conflict with it. Nevertheless, the Amish have established and managed to hold on to a community life that is supportive, rewarding and predictable and that meets the needs of its members.

Not What I Will

The Amish emphasis on being a distinctive Christian community and the submission and yieldedness to it that is necessary is supported in scripture. Being distinctively Christian as a community requires being set apart and different from the world. For example, Paul in Romans 12:2

states, *"And do not be conformed to this world, but be transformed by the renewing of your mind, that you may prove what is that good and acceptable and perfect will of God."* Individual believers are to offer their life as a sacrifice and a community of believers is to do the same. The Amish seek to ensure that their attitudes, thoughts, feelings, and actions are in line with the sacrifice they are making. As the individual and the community are transformed they come to approve and desire God's will, not their own.

Peter also talks about the unique nature of Christian believers stating, *"But you are a chosen generation, a royal priesthood, a holy nation, His own special people, that you may proclaim the praises of Him who called you out of darkness into His marvelous light;"* (1 Peter 2:9). In writing this he was exhorting the believers of his time to live holy lives, different from the corrupted world around them. As a community they were to be distinctively different and and through their actions and words able to declare the praises of God to others. The Amish emphasize actions more than words and their actions have proven to be an attractive draw to those who want to know more about what makes them special—that being their devotion to God.

Being set apart from the rest of the world the Amish seek to strengthen the community by following scriptural guidance. Acts 2:42 is a example, *"And they continued steadfastly in the apostles' doctrine and fellowship, in the breaking of bread, and in prayers."* A community of believers, according to such scripture, is to continue adhering to the gospel passed down by Christ to the apostles and to remain in continual fellowship with one another. Part of this fellowship includes sharing meals together and praying together. Many Christian communities do these things, but the Amish generally do so with great dedication and devotion. They seek to prevent the world from intruding on the purity and practice of their faith.

Another example is Philippians 2:4, which combines the injunction to yield to one another with that of community, *"Let each of you look out not only for his own interests, but also for the interests of others."* Preoccupation with self is a sin, but showing concerning for the interests of others is an expression of love and humility. The Amish are well known for their willingness to attend to the interests of not only other Amish, but also those outside the plain community who are in need.

The Amish willingness to yield and submit to God and others is modeled on the example of Christ. Perhaps no better scripture encapsules this willingness than Jesus' words just before His crucifixion in Matthew 26:39: *"He went a little farther and fell on His face, and prayed, saying, "O My Father, if it is possible, let this cup pass from Me; nevertheless, not as I will, but as You will."* The significance of this scripture is that Jesus submitted His will to the will of the Father. Submission is the core of man's relationship with God and is the will and command of God. Unfortunately, from the very beginning man has refused to submit as when Adam and Eve revolted against God and followed their own desires. Submission has been and continues to be a major problem for humankind. However, believers are called to not only believe in the Lord but to submit and follow Him.

Submission is also the key for harmony and unity in human relationships. As mentioned above in Philippians 2:4 we are to submit our will to the need to look out for the interests of others. People would have no need for conflict or disharmony if we were all more concerned about others than we were for ourselves.

Biblical submission is motivated by faith, hope and love and results in self-sacrifice. As Hebrews 11:1 states *"Now faith is the substance of things hoped for, the evidence of things not seen."* We don't always see the benefit of submitting to God and others, but our faith allows us to believe that in the long term what we give up now will be for a result much better than we can imagine. Christians willingly submit and endure suffering as a result of our heavenly hope in and love of God.

Submission is also based on our understanding of our interdependence on one another. For example, Romans 14:7 states, *"For none of us lives to himself, and no one dies to himself"* and 1 Corinthians 11:11confirms *"Nevertheless, neither is man independent of woman, nor woman independent of man, in the Lord."* The world in which we live tells us to minimize our dependence upon others and maximize our own independence. God teaches us to recognize our dependence on others and surrender our independence.

Believers need to recognize that submission should be part of every relationship they have. We are first to be submissive to God (Ephesians 5:21-22); then we are to be mutually submissive to other believers (Romans 12:10).

Husbands and wives are to submit to one another (1 Corinthians 1:11); and finally Christians are to be submissive to all (1 Peter 2:13-17).

Purposeful Community

The Amish put such great emphasis on building and maintaining a close Christian community for a purpose. They know that such bonds will help each of them individually and collectively better adhere to their distinctive faith and practice. While others, such as you and I, don't reside in or benefit from the Amish way of community, nevertheless we can borrow some helpful principles from their example and strengthen our own bonds of community with God and others.

- *Eliminate your addiction to the artificial community that has taken over your life.* My wife and I endured Hurricane Katrina while living about 70 miles from the Mississippi Coast. The primary form of damage in our area was from the countless number of trees that were blown over in our area known as the Pine Belt. With the collapsing of whole forests of trees also came the loss of electrical power for a long period of time. We learned that when we don't have TV, and we don't have the internet, and when we don't have telephone service, we naturally seek out other ways of connecting with others. Neighbors started coming out of their homes and helping one another. They began visiting in each other's houses and sitting and talking in rocking chairs on porches. They actually started to interact face-to-face. Unfortunately, immediately after power was restored everything changed. Neighbors began staying in their homes as they returned to their TV or computer. Visiting dramatically declined and the streets and porches became barren once again.

Recently, I read an article about a middle age female executive at Facebook who was positioned high up in the leadership chain. Over time she began to realize there was something missing in her life. Through Facebook she had hundreds if not thousands of "friends," though they were mostly shallow and artificial in nature. In real life her personal relationships were not what she desired. Finally, she resigned from the company and moved to a small west Texas town. She unplugged her Facebook account and has begun developing deeper personal relationships ever since.

If you want real community, you must first rid yourself or limit those things in your life that are preventing this. Whether the hindrance is the television, telephone, social media, video games or other distractions, following the example of the Amish in this area can only help.

- *Allow God's word to replace those artificial forms of community you have eliminated from your life.* The forms of artificial community that filled a need in your life, albeit poorly, need to be replaced by something that will help you achieve real community with God and others. The only thing that can help you to do this is God's Word. God's Word contains all the keys you need to have true fellowship with Him and other believers. God's relationship with His children is based on love, compassion and mercy if we are willing to receive it. Likewise, when our relationship with others is based on love, compassion and mercy we will experience a sense of greater openness and community which will allow our relationships to blossom. Relationships based on anything else will never reach the full potential of community that God intended.

- *Make growing in community an intentional act.* Someone by the name of Liberty Hyde Bailey once said "A garden requires patient labor and attention. Plants do not grow merely to satisfy ambitions or to fulfill good intentions. They thrive because someone expended effort on them." We can all wish for a greater sense of community with God and others in our life, but nothing will come of our wishes if we do not expend effort to achieve this desire. If you want to have greater, more personal communion with God and others then you need to intentionally act to make it so. You must approach God through studying His Word, praying to him regularly, worshipping Him, and waiting on Him. You cannot expect to have a close relationship with God if you are not doing your part. Likewise, if you desire greater community with other believers then you must intentionally approach them, spend time with them, get to know them, fellowship with them, and help them with their needs. By spending this time you will find that your relationships become deeper and more meaningful.

- *Master the spiritual practice of giving up self to God and others.* Each of us by nature is selfish. It's a fact of life. Some more so than others. Still, our fallen nature doesn't prevent us from striving to become and do better. We all have the capability to corral our selfish nature and give up our desires and needs in favor of those of God and others. This can take place with determination, practice and maturity. The more you practice giving up self the easier you will find it to live this way on a daily basis.

Work

Work holds a special place in the lives of the Amish and rightly so for work is one of the central bonds that hold Amish family and community together. Work to the Amish is a "sacred ritual" with spiritual dimensions.[28] Idleness, the opposite of work, is understood by the Amish to be Satan's tool to lead people into sin. The Amish remind each other of King David who instead of joining his army in battle chose to remain behind in his palace idly passing the time. While doing so on his rooftop he spied the beautiful yet married woman Bathsheba with whom he committed adultery. With such biblical reminders the Amish scorn idleness and promote industry, labor, and work.

The value of work is instilled in Amish children from the earliest ages. As early as age four Amish children begin to assist their parents and are given limited responsibility at the age of six.[29] Such tasks as feeding the chickens, gathering eggs, driving the horses are common for boys as is learning cooking and housekeeping for girls. Many Amish children are even given an animal such as a calf or heifer, which they name and are responsible to care for. Once the animal matures and maybe even produces its own offspring, the child can sell it and the proceeds placed into a savings account. Children are taught the importance of work not just because it is a virtue for them to learn, but often because of economic necessity.[30] The work efforts of Amish children frequently contribute in a direct manner to the economic well-being of the family.

It has been pointed out that the Amish have an economy of production, not consumption.[31] Work is not a means to enable conspicuous consumption, like it is for many modern individuals. Work is to provide for the basic needs of the family. Work for the Amish is often hands-on, difficult and dirty, but it is also meaningful and helps to build community. It is also considered a calling from God, not a career. Because Amish work is hands-on it helps to promote a pragmatic mentality that values the practical things in life rather than the abstract and theoretical.

While Amish work is meaningful within the larger context of their spiritual and physical lives, the Amish do not look to work to give them meaning. Within modern society many individuals look to their job or career as that activity that defines who they are and provides the primary meaning in their life. Since the idea of God is often peripheral or non-existent in their lives, they naturally turn to their work and what they can achieve through it. When their expectations don't align with their actual job experience they find themselves frustrated and depressed. The Amish enjoy their work but are careful not to make work and their achievements a god itself.

Within the "Rules for a Godly Life," which the Amish strive to abide by, several statements deal directly with work. For example, one sstates the following:

Do not attempt supporting yourself in any occupation forbidden by God. For to what advantage is wealth won at the expense of your soul? Matthew 16:26. Even though you may make great temporal gains through dishonesty, you will thereby forfeit the blessing of a clear conscience. Who can bear the burden of a disturbed, nagging conscience? Be diligent, therefore as was the Apostle Paul, always taking pains to have a clear conscience towards God and towards men. Acts 24:16.

Still another warns against the dangers of idleness:

Detest idleness as a pillow of Satan and a cause of all sorts of wickedness, and be diligent in your appointed tasks that you not be found idle. Satan has great power over the idle, to lead them into many sins. King David was idle on the rooftop of his house when he

fell into adultery. II Samuel 11:2-5.

Finally, another helps the Amish to place the proper perspective on those worldly possessions they may gain by their work:

No one is his own master, only a steward of

that which is in his care. Therefore give of

your goods to the poor and needy, wisely,

willingly, and heartily. II Corinthians 9:7.

One of the most basic forms of work for the Amish is plowing the field. Working the earth and growing crops is revered by the Amish as a means to draw closer to God. For this reason and others the Amish have eschewed most modern machinery and still use the horse and plow. The work is harder and dirtier, but the rewards of enjoying God's creation and sensing His presence is worth the sacrifice. The Amish recognize that many modern conveniences effectively serve to disconnect people from

God's handiwork and from God Himself. They also serve to glorify the inventiveness of man over the creativeness of God. By continuing to conduct work in the most basic means possible, the Amish are able to continue to recognize His work and give Him the glory.

Work is truly a blessing. It is not simply drudgery to be avoided. The Amish see work as an opportunity, not as a problem. They see work as an opportunity to commune with and glorify God, not to laud their own efforts and achievements. The Amish see work as a chance to build character, not as a way to enrich themselves in an endless competition with others. Work is a blessing given by God.

Work Brings a Profit

The Bible is full of scripture describing work, encouraging work, promoting the benefits of work, discouraging evil works and so on. Work obviously takes an important place in the eyes of God and believers are encouraged to work.

Idleness on the other hand is rejected and disparaged in no uncertain terms. The earliest scriptures in the Bible describe the creative work of God and how it spanned over six days. As God surveyed His work he saw what He had made and it was good. Then in Genesis 2:2-3 scripture reads, *"And on the seventh day God ended His work which He had done, and He rested on the seventh day from all His work which He had done. Then God blessed the seventh day and sanctified it, because in it He rested from all His work which God had created and made."* These scriptures reveal that God is a God of work and the work He does is good. His example is the example for all of us to follow. Believers should be a working people of good works.

As many Amish have found, work is to be enjoyed. Ecclesiastes 3:22 says, *"So I perceived that nothing is better than that a man should rejoice in his own works, for that is his heritage. For who can bring him to see what will happen after him?"* Matthew Henry in his commentary on the Bible offers helpful insight on the blessing of work and the need to enjoy it:

> "There is nothing better, as to this world, nothing better to be had out of our wealth and honour, than that a man should rejoice in his own works, that is, (1.) Keep a clear conscience, and never admit iniquity into *the place of* righteousness. Let every man prove his own work, and approve himself to God in it, so shall he have rejoicing in himself alone. Let him not get nor keep anything but what he can rejoice in. (2.) Live a cheerful life. If God have prospered the work of our hands unto us, let us rejoice in it, and take the comfort of it, and not make it a burden to ourselves and leave others the joy of it; for that is our portion, not the portion of our

souls… but it is the portion of the body; that only which we enjoy is ours out of this world; it is taking what is to be had and making the best of it, and the reason is because none can give us a sight of what shall be after us, either who shall have our estates or what use they will make of them."

One of the most meaningful ways to engage in work is directly with the use of our own hands. The apostle Paul is well known for the fact that along with preaching God's word he also bi-vocationally supported himself as a tentmaker. In 1 Corinthians 4:12 he states, *"And we labor, working with our own hands,"* and again in 1 Thessalonians 4:11 he advises his readers to *"…aspire to lead a quiet life, to mind your own business, and to work with your own hands, as we commanded you…"* Working with one's own hands as described here is a demonstration of love because a self-supporting person is not a burden on others. Working with one's own hands also reminds the worker of God as they shape and form His creation for their purposes. The Amish also recognize that manual labor builds character, endurance and perseverance.

Work, particularly manual labor, brings a satisfaction with it that other forms of more hands-ff work does not. An owner of a company may see the financial rewards of his business, but he may not actually see the physical results of it. This is not to denigrate the efforts of those who own companies, but if asked, many would say the most satisfying times in their work life was when they had their hands literally involved in the work process. Proverbs 12:11 serves as a reminder of the benefits of direct manual labor, *"He who tills his land will be satisfied with bread, but he who follows frivolity is devoid of understanding."* Sometimes we find ourselves having taken our hands off the plow and now chasing frivolities. Chasing frivolities in life will never bring the sense of satisfaction and meaning that work does.

Idleness, the opposite of work is roundly condemned in God's Word and examples of its consequences given. Proverbs is particularly replete with warnings against idleness or laziness. For example, *"The desire of the lazy man kills him, For his hands refuse to labor"* (Proverbs 21:25) and *"The lazy man will not plow because of winter; He will beg during harvest and have nothing"* (Proverbs 20:4). Jesus even tells a parable about some servants who were given talents to use by their master but one does nothing with his, he does not put them to work. He is condemned by his master and the little that he had was taken away (Matthew 25:14-29). Jesus told this parable illustrating the fact that believers should be productively at work for God. Then there is the story of David, mentioned earlier, who did not go out to battle with his army. While he idly strolled on his palace rooftop he was led into temptation and committed adultery. His idleness set in motion a whole chain of events throughout his life that led to death within his family and much grief.

Clearly work is considered good in the eyes of God and idleness wicked. Work brings with it many benefits that are physical, emotional and spiritual in nature. Engaging in productive work is following in the example of the Lord. Idleness can lead to temptation filled situations that are hard to resist for believer and unbeliever alike. Work that is manual in nature offers its own special advantages over work that is accomplished through others or is immaterial in nature.

Meaningful Work

Work, if approached correctly, can be an enjoyable and meaningful activity for every person. Engaging in work is the example set by the Creator and the command he gave in Genesis 1:28: "*God blessed them and said to them, 'Be fruitful and increase in number; fill the earth and subdue it."* "Filling the earth and subduing it" is a large portion of our work. But we must always keep in mind the Creator who gave us the work in the first place and how it relates to Him. Consider the following suggestions to help you in maintaining a proper balance between your goals in work and what God desires.

- *When you work work for the glory of God.* Too often our work becomes about us. Work becomes about what we can accomplish, what rewards we will receive, what recognition will come our way. This is not as God intended. Everything that we do should be done for the glory of God. First Corinthians 10:31 tells us *"Therefore… whatever you do, do all to the glory of God."* Glorifying God is not just meant for worship on Sunday mornings. Glorifying God should be involved in whatever we do. The story is told of a woman who cleaned the same office building for many years. When asked how she endured the drudgery of doing the same chores day in and day out, she replied, "It's not drudgery. You see, I'm working for the King and He's pleased along with others when I do my best." Work is central to what God has prepared for us so that He might bless us and make us a blessing to the world. Our work matters and it matters to God. Like the woman who seemed to be doing drudge work, by giving our best for the glory of God we can make a difference in our life and the lives of those around us.

- *Use a portion of the fruits of your labor to serve the needs of others.* Our society has become so materialistic in outlook that people's mentality towards possessions has become distorted. Many people think that their main objective in life is to collect as many expensive material possessions as they can before their life expires. In the final analysis, they discover that their pursuit of possessions is purposeless and empty. True happiness comes from a willingness to use the fruits of our labor to serve the needs of others. When we are able to help someone else we are not only being obedient to God's word, but we also fulfill a deeper need each of us has to care for our fellow man. Luke 6:38 is a wonderful verse that describes the blessing of giving, *"Give, and it will be given to you: good measure, pressed down, shaken together, and running over will be put into your bosom. For with the same measure that you use, it will be measured back to you."* The principle Jesus is trying to get across here is that he who sows will reap. This is referring less to reaping physical rewards and more to reaping those of a spiritual nature.

- *Incorporate some form of manual labor into your life.* Modern work has become increasingly mental in nature and less manual. This is a modern phenomena primarily associated with the 20th and 21st century. Prior to this time, even if you were an elite it would not be uncommon for you to be engaging in some form of manual labor. The Amish recognize the benefit and blessing of manual labor and how it helps to keep them closer to God. Getting our hands dirty through manual labor has a humbling quality to it that helps bring us back to reality no matter what our position in life. Perhaps you have seen the television show where the CEO of a large national company agrees to incognito join the ranks of his lowest level employees. In doing so, he or she typically ends up doing some form of manual labor that their company specializes in. As the show progresses, the CEO usually comes to a better realization of the needs and stresses of his employees and develops greater compassion for them. He also comes to appreciate the nature of the work their company does to a greater extent. Incorporating some form of manual labor into your life will bring you unexpected benefits and blessings and more humbleness before the Lord.

- *Seek to eliminate risky idleness from your life.* There is a difference between rest and idleness. Rest is what you do to take stock of and recover from work you have been doing. Idleness is very simply avoiding work. David appears to have been avoiding work when he stayed home at his palace rather than going out with his army. In many ways the society in which we live rewards those who pursue idleness by providing their basic needs for them without requiring anything in return. Christian believers should avoid taking from certain programs if they are designed in such a way as to encourage greater idleness in them. There is nothing wrong with accepting help, but accepting help that will demotivate you to actively work is spiritually harmful. Those times when we are idle are the times we are most likely to be tempted into behaviors that we know are wrong. Take stock of those times you have given in to temptations and determine if idleness played a role. There is a good chance that it did. Make a choice to eliminate idleness from your life and you will find, like the Amish, that you are better off for it.

Afterword

Most people want to be a better person than they are now. When people observe the Amish and their way of life, they often think it would be nice to be more like them. The reality is though that very few will every totally change their life in such a way as to become Amish. But many *are* willing to make small changes in emulation of the Amish that can make a difference. The seven core values described in the preceding pages can help you do that. You simply have to start with a willingness to change. In looking back over each of the seven core values I would suggest the following to help you in your journey.

First, don't be content with where your life is now. You probably have already recognized areas of your life after reading over the seven core values that you think, "Hey, I would like my life to be more that way." Then you may have passed over it with little further thought. I encourage you to reconsider these thoughts and think how much better your life could be if you actually tried to implement these. Once you do that you will probably not continue to be content with your life as is.

Second, make a commitment to change. Let's say one of the areas you want to change is you want a simpler life. You want to get back to the basics without all the complications of excess material goods and activities that moderns seem to gravitate towards. Evaluate your current situation, set a goal for change and then commit yourself to it. Once you start to rid your life of these extras, you will find a greater sense of peace and contentedness.

Third, continue to house clean. While you may start with one of the core values continue to move on to the other ones that seem particularly relevant to your life and what you need. The most enduring life changes are often those that occur gradually. After making these changes it is my hope you will enjoy the blessings of living the Amish way.

---

[1] Donald B. Kraybill and others, *The Amish Way: Patient Faith in a Perilous*

World (San Francisco: Jossey Bass, 2010), 126.

[2] D. Kraybill and others, *The Amish Way.*

[3] Joe Wittmer, *The Gentle People: An Inside View of Amish Life* (Wittmer Books, 2010), 4.

[4] Donald B Kraybill, *The Riddle of Amish Culture, Rev.* (Baltimore: Johns Hopkins University Press), 45.

[5] D. Kraybill, *The Riddle of Amish Culture, Rev.*

[6] D. Kraybill and others, *The Amish Way,* 124,

[7] D. Kraybill, *The Riddle of Amish Culture, Rev., 210.*

[8] Elmo Stoll, *Strangers and Pilgrims: Why We Live Simply* (Aylmer, ON: Pathway Publishers, 2008) 8.

[9] D. Kraybill and others, *The Amish Way,* 35.

[10] D. Kraybill, *The Riddle of Amish Culture, Rev.,58.*

[11] Ibid.

[12] D. Kraybill and others, *The Amish Way,* 134.

[13] Ibid. 43.

[14] Ibid. 111.

[15] D. Kraybill, *The Riddle of Amish Culture, Rev.* 123.

[16] D. Kraybill and others, *The Amish Way,* 39.

[17] Dordrect Confession of Faith, 1632.

[18] D. Kraybill, *The Riddle of Amish Culture, Rev.* 137.

[19] John A. Hostetler, *Amish Society* (Baltimore: The Johns Hopkins University Press), 73.

[20] D. Kraybill, *The Riddle of Amish Culture, Rev.* 189.

[21] Ibid.

[22] D. Kraybill and others, *The Amish Way,* 35.

[23] D. Kraybill, *The Riddle of Amish Culture, Rev.* 150.

[24] John A. Hostetler, *Amish Society, 4th ed.* (Baltimore: Johns Hopkins University Press), 221-222.

[25] Ibid. 15.

[26] D. Kraybill and others, *The Amish Way,* 53.

[27] Ibid.

[28] D. Kraybill, *The Riddle of Amish Culture, Rev.* 46.

[29] J. Hostetler, *Amish Society, 4th ed.,* 158.

[30] D. Kraybill and others, *The Amish Way,* 102.

[31] D. Kraybill, *The Riddle of Amish Culture, Rev.* 46.

Printed in Great Britain
by Amazon

37869391R00078